T0132077

Miss Diagnosed

By: C. L. McGinnes

Illustrated by: Jeanne Ee Wei Yen

Copyright © 2019 C. L. McGinnes.
Interior and cover art credit: Jeanne Ee Wei Yen

All rights reserved. No part of this book may be used or reproduced by any means, graphic, electronic, or mechanical, including photocopying, recording, taping or by any information storage retrieval system without the written permission of the author except in the case of brief quotations embodied in critical articles and reviews.

WestBow Press books may be ordered through booksellers or by contacting:

WestBow Press
A Division of Thomas Nelson & Zondervan
1663 Liberty Drive
Bloomington, IN 47403
www.westbowpress.com
1 (866) 928-1240

Because of the dynamic nature of the Internet, any web addresses or links contained in this book may have changed since publication and may no longer be valid. The views expressed in this work are solely those of the author and do not necessarily reflect the views of the publisher, and the publisher hereby disclaims any responsibility for them.

Any people depicted in stock imagery provided by Getty Images are models, and such images are being used for illustrative purposes only.
Certain stock imagery © Getty Images.

ISBN: 978-1-9736-6304-1 (sc)
ISBN: 978-1-9736-6305-8 (e)

Library of Congress Control Number: 2019907102

Print information available on the last page.

WestBow Press rev. date: 6/10/2019

WestBow
PRESS®
A DIVISION OF THOMAS NELSON
& ZONDERVAN

To my God, thank you for always loving
me and keeping your promises.

To Martin, thank you for always supporting me in all
my endeavors. I couldn't do it all without you.

To Mom and Marti, your constant support and
encouragement has kept me going and strong.

To Cannon and Harper, may you always know
exactly who you are and whose you are.

I am Miss Diagnosed

And I am here to set you straight

You are not of this world

And neither is your fate

They place a label on your life

And tell you who you'll be

But just remember little one

You're more than what they see

A diagnosis can't define you
It cannot hold you back

Because the God that loves you so

Makes up for all the lack

He fills in holes

And changes DNA

He can even heal a brain

In His own amazing way

He takes all our hurts

And makes them something new

And all the things that were stolen

He gives back to you

It has been written

He'll never leave or forsake

So just rely on Him my dear

He's never, ever late

God says that you're beautiful

And guess what so do I

No one can place a limit on you

When the limit is the sky

And if you forget who you are

Just look towards the tree

Because of what Christ did for you You can know your identity

Printed in the United States
By Bookmasters